The Weeping of the Sunflower

Emilee Robb

BookLeaf
Publishing

India | USA | UK

For my students; know that you have all the power in the world at your fingertips and do not be afraid to use it; what you have to say matters even if you think no one is listening.

PREFACE

This collection travels to you from the deepness of my heart and contains words that I never planned to share. These words were a let out of emotions ranging from sorrow so strong its painful, to happiness so grand it glows, to an anger so deep that it brings tears to the surface. Be careful with my heart that you hold here in your hands.

Writing Is...

Writing is an act of expression.

When you write, you are able to get emotions
from your soul into the hearts of others.
When you write, you are able to extinguish your
worries and fears out of your mind and on to a
page.
When you write, you are laying out a piece of
your soul for all the world to see.

Writing is an act of power.

When you write, you are claiming the words
found deep within yourself.
When you write, you are giving voice and
agency to the matters of your mind.
When you write, you are making people listen.

Writing is emotional.
Writing is frustrating.
Writing is personal.
Writing is a right.
Writing is a privilege.

Words

I struggle to find words that have yet to be said,
as the phrases of the greats mingle; stuck within
my head.
I am no Shakespeare; I have no sonnets of love
to share.
No Maya Angelou with tales of sorrow and
strength to show and bare.
I could never compete with the rhymes and
meter of Seuss,
so why even write when it seems there is no use.
For all I know there are no things left to say,
no new meanings, thoughts, or feelings for my
pencil to convey.

I struggle to find words that have yet to be said,
as the phrases of the greats mingle; stuck within
my head.
It's comforting to imagine that they once felt
this, too-
before their words found their way to me and to
you.
So I'll continue to write, though struggle I may,
for my words will mean something to someone,
somewhere, someday.

A Flower's Tears

For change to occur,
we must mourn of the past
the times that are gone,
and not coming back.
The sadness of life
creates hope for tomorrow.
Flowers cry too, just like us.
But instead of tears
their petals fall,
thus creating the beautiful new.

The Reason

They say people come into our lives for a
reason,
so I've been trying to figure out yours
when it seems all you did in my heart was create
a lesion,
and left me locking up all of my doors.

There are times when I forget that you even
exist,
and times when I remember every little part.
Times when the feelings of lonesome begin to
subsist,
then times when your memory pulls upon my
heart.

I'll never understand why our paths had to cross,
when there was nothing about us that ever stood
a chance.
Was it simply to know the feel of love loss,
or a wondrous dream of which we only received
a glance?

They say people come into our lives for a
reason,
so I'll keep trying to figure out yours.

Trees

I wonder how it would feel to be a friend of the
trees.

Would they help me take cover from the storms
in my mind?
Would they shade me from the sorrow of this
world?
Would they block the winds that try to blow my
life right off its tracks?
And would they give me roots for when my
stubborn soul starts to wander?

I'm sure they would be there, no matter what the
weather,
and stay grounded, strong, and true when others
have often left
I bet they would act as a fierce earthly tether,
and of their strength and support I shall not be
bereft.

I wonder how I could be a friend of the trees?

The Sun's Haikus

The sun rises high
as we bid the moon goodbye,
welcoming the day.

Warm rays from above
uncover shadows from dark,
making way for hope.

Though she cannot stay
any longer than a day,
again she will rise.

The Path

Along the river runs a path just wide enough for
two,
where children run and elderly stroll in search of
the perfect view.
Along the way you'll find a bench meant to take
a rest.
To calm your mind with nature, truly is the best.
When you begin to walk again, take note of any
sound.
As the nature of the world plays greatly all
around.
Arriving at the clearing, you will look upon the
lake.
The view you have been searching for; your
breath it shall take.
In this moment you will see a place where the
heavens meet the earth;
a place where beauty is shown for everything it's
worth.
Along the river runs a path, just wide enough for
two,
that leads to a wondrous place with an
unbeatable view.

A Voice Unseized

It's as if I open my mouth and the winds steal my
sound.
They carry it away to lands far from here
until they dump it in the sea so not a soul on
Earth can hear.
I would ask the wind why, but I'm afraid of the
reason.
Maybe it's better to be silent than to use my
voice as a beacon.
But what if one day those waves echo back
more powerful a voice than any could attack?
What if one day, somewhere out there, someone
who needs them hears those words loud and
clear?
So I'll continue to shout despite the thief in the
breeze
for my voice is something meaningful that no
one can seize.

Friend for a Lifetime

What would those little girls we used to be think
of you and of me?

From pigtails and ball caps, to dry shampoo and
rushing out the door to make it to work on time.

From slumber parties filled with too many kids
and laughter echoing throughout the house,
to girls' night out without another soul around,
still laughing til it hurts.

From playing dolls and school in your comfy
little basement,
to motherhood and a teaching salary that just
barely pays the bills.

Though every single ounce of our lives has
changed, there is one part that has always
remained.
You are the call I make when my emotions
become too much.
You are the ears that listen as I pour out my soul
and the burdens that come with it.
You are the comforting words that pull me back
from the ledge.

You are the friend that will forever be more
family instead.

The years have changed us more than we know,
yet sometimes it seems not that long ago.
Those little girls we were still live in our souls,
and they cheer us on together as we strive
towards all our goals.

Mountain of Fear

Fear is a funny thing.
It can manipulate the most normal element and
create an impassable mountain that your mind,
soul, and body cannot fathom overcoming.

Fear does not play favorites.
Even the so-called fearless hide those barriers
deep within their souls in the hopes that those
feelings will fail to escape.

Fear can be debilitating.
It can freeze you to a place; a moment; a person;
a memory.
You do not even need to be in the presence of
that which you fear in order to feel the twisting
of emotions strong inside you.

Fear is powerful.
Fear is draining.
Fear is that scream stuck in the back of your
throat begging to be let out.

Fear is conquerable.
Conquering is power.

Power is climbing that mountain inside of your
soul and finding solace on the other side of fear.
Fear is a funny thing.

Forgotten Way

Deep within the woods lay a path long forgotten.
The overgrowth hides what used to be
a way of connecting you to me.

Though many years removed I've been,
I still know the way by heart;
this untended trail all that's keeping us apart.

I cannot bear this distance,
so I will begin to clear a way
in the hopes that we will be together, connected
again someday.

Halfway along the path, I notice the overgrowth
trimmed back.
I begin to cry just a little,
as I see you have met me in the middle.

Second Choice

I will always be his second choice,
no matter what I do.
I will always be his second choice,
when the choice is me or you.

Though he claims to love me more,
I know it's just for show
because the second you come through the door,
out it all of his promises go.

So, I'll stand here as he chooses you time and
time again
til he sees that you, dear alcohol, could never be
his friend.

A Sense of Humor

You looked at me and laughed at the jokes your
friends made about me.

I have no sense of humor, you say.
Lighten up, they're just having fun.

Their joy should not come at the expense of my
self worth.
Their joy should not come at the expense of
young girls who have fought to be thought of as
equals in your world.
Their joy should not come at the expense of my
tears.

I have worked my whole life to become the
young woman I now am, and with one joke, one
laugh, you tear apart the very foundation upon
which I stand.

So no, I do not find humor in your misogynistic
mind.
No, I do not find humor in your pitiful lines.
But I do find humor in the fact that you think
your world is anything like mine.

A Stranger

I wonder what a stranger would think if they
woke up in my life for a day.

Would they laugh at the four alarms set for my
morning wake up beeping,
or would they recognize the response to the
nagging anxiety of oversleeping?
Would they see my chipped nail polish as a sign
they need redone,
or would they pick up the nervous habit before
the day is done?
Would they figure out my necklace is much
more than decoration,
but a comforting physical tether when my mind
needs space for evacuation?

I wonder what a stranger would think if they
woke up in my life for a day.
Would they see the parts of me that I keep
hidden away,
or am I good at burying them so that people will
stay?

The Gardener

Every day she brings the water to help the
flowers bloom.
She turns the pots this way and that to ensure
each petal sees the light.
When frost comes on quickly, she brings the
flowers into her room,
to ensure that their beauty can last throughout
the night.

She has dedicated many hours tending to her
flowers,
leading to colorful petals rivaled by none.
At her skillset with these treasures, even Mother
Nature cowers,
and her approval the Gardener has won.

One day this Gardener will go
and leave her plants behind;
their petals left for another to sow,
though none will be as kind.

Lost Emotion

I woke today feeling like a stranger in my own
life.
I am surrounded by the same four walls that
have sheltered me since toddler years, yet lost is
all I feel;like a soul trapped in another's routine,
following along with what I think I should be
doing.
I pass by the people of my life and know that
they are there, but feel no pull to be near them or
to even care.
I feel alone, yet I am surrounded by the
remnants of this other me.
It's as if the tether between my heart and my
mind has been disconnected somewhere along
the line.
I see this all familiar life; I feel nothing.
I wonder to myself, "Would I rather bask forever
in indifference or reconnect that binding tether
of emotion to open the gates and risk the pain to
receive the joy that's intertwined?"

If I Left

If I left today, would they even care or notice I
was gone?
Would they mourn what they have lost, or
simply just move on?
Would they remember any piece of me, any
aspect of who I was,
or would they forget my existence as it seems
everyone eventually does?

Sometimes I wish I could disappear to see if
they would care.
But I don't, for if they didn't my heart painfully
would tear.
So I'll remain here in their story as the character
on the side;
the one who never conquers all, but is there
because they tried.

Just Like Her

All my life I was haunted by a series of six
words strung together.
"You are just like your mother."
A simple phrase,yet it felt like a deflation of the
whole of my individuality;
a suffocation of the new and unique identity I
was striving to create.

All my life I was haunted by a series of six
words strung together,
though somewhere along the way the haunting
turned to guiding, and the words transformed
from shadows looming overhead to light
illuminating the path of this life I so desired.

"You are just like your mother."
A strong woman who refuses to be defined by
any person or standard.

"You are just like your mother."
A caring soul who places others on her back to
carry them to calmer, happier shores.

"You are just like your mother."

A provider who works tirelessly so that not a
person in her care, young or old, wants for
anything.

"You are just like your mother."
A beacon of light when the darkness becomes
too powerful to bear all alone.

"You are just like your mother."
And just like her is everything that I am striving
to become.

Goodbye

Today we said goodbye, even though you have
yet to leave.
These will be the longest yet most fleeting days
until you are at peace.
These days of waiting while reminiscing;
these days of silent tears that serve as a
premonition of the floods soon to overtake our
very core;
these days of laughter that have brought together
a family once distanced by pride and
misunderstanding;
these days are more for us than you, as we
selfishly squeeze the last ounces of love from
the beautiful soul that we have grown with.

Today we said goodbye, even though you have
yet to leave.
This is our way of showing you that everything's
okay.
We know you have been ready and waiting for a
while,
and though we may never truly feel that same
readiness to let you go,
today is the day you start your journey home.

Army of the Stars

One hundred billion stars find themselves
together in our galaxy,
each with their own light to shine.
Though some may prove to be brighter than
others, their uniqueness is what gives them
power.

Few stars are appointed the messengers of the
sky,
shooting from one place to another spreading
tales as they go.

Even fewer stars are bound by invisible tethers
to one another and bare the remarkable
responsibility of painting pictures in the still of
the night.

An army of celestial bodies serves in the
darkness of the night,
providing relief from the fear of the unknown;
shining light on all that is hidden;
guiding lost souls home.

One hundred billion stars find themselves in our
galaxy,
striving to ensure a world forever void of
darkness.

A Flower in the Dark

In the dark of the night, the flower turns down protecting itself from whatever may lurk in the distance.
In the dark of the night, the flower goes unnoticed; hiding its beauty from being seen.
In the dark of the night, the flower is forgotten amidst the fear of the otherwise unknown.

Yet, soon the sun rises in the quiet hours of the morning; bringing with it the exposure of the petals.
In the light of the sun, the flower basks in the warmth the morning star has to offer.
In the light of the sun, the flower exposes its own beauty to the scrutiny of the world.
In the light of the sun, the flower has no fear of the unknown along the horizon.

You, my darling, are the flower.
Though you hide in the fear of the darkness, the sun will soon rise and bathe you in the warmth of its light.
And when this happens, your heart will open as the petals, exposing the beauty that lies in your soul for all the world to see.